Magyu Tsalung and Tummo

Teachings by Drubdra Khenpo Tsultrim Tenzin

according to the

*Clear explanations on the daily practice of tsalung and tummo
from the Mother Tantra, which is both an excellent medicine
for healing hundreds of diseases
and the essential elixir of immortality*

ཉིན་རེའི་འཚོ་བའི་རྣང་དུ་ཉེ་བར་མཁོ་བའི་གསང་སྔགས་
མ་རྒྱུད་ཀྱི་རྩ་རླུང་གཏུམ་མོའི་
ལག་ལེན་གསལ་བར་བཏད་པ་ནད་བརྒྱ་སེལ་བའི་སྨན་མཆོག་
འཆི་མེད་ཚེ་ཡི་བདུད་རྩི་ཞེས་བྱ་བ་བཞུགས།

Transcribed and edited by
Carol Ermakova & Dmitry Ermakov
Illustrations by Yungdrung Rabten

Public Series A

Illustrations by Yungdrung Rabten.
Photos by Carol Ermakova.
Magyu thangka photo courtesy Christophe Moulin.

Published by
Foundation for the Preservation of Yungdrung Bön

ISBN: 978-0-9955368-4-5

FOUNDATION FOR
THE PRESERVATION
OF YUNGDRUNG BÖN
གཡུང་དྲུང་བོན་ཉར་ཚགས་རིག་མཛོད།
WWW.YUNGDRUNGBON.CO.UK

FPYB is a charitable non-profit
organization. All proceeds from
sales are reinvested into
ongoing projects. Registered
Charity (England and Wales)
№ 1173639

Contents

Foreword

This book contains a daily practice manual on the *yoga* of winds, channels, inner heat and physical exercises extracted by Drubdra Khenpo Tsultrim Tenzin from the Mother Tantra of Yungdrung Bön, the spiritual tradition of Tibet which stems from the Central Asian Buddha Tönpa Shenrab Miwo who predates the more widely known Indian Buddha Shakyamuni by thousands of years.

While these techniques were previously reserved for those initiated into the Mother Tantra, Drubdra Khenpo has decided to share his daily practice with a wider audience because these methods have the potential to bring profound benefits not only for the development of meditation but also for health.

This book is an edited transcript of oral teachings given by Drubdra Khenpo Tsultrim Tenzin at the Foundation for the Preservation of Yungdrung Bön, North Pennines, UK, in November 2017. We have chosen this format rather than a word by word scholarly translation of the text he taught from,

ཉིན་རེའི་འཚོ་བའི་ནང་དུ་ཉེ་བར་མཁོ་བའི་གསང་སྔགས་མ་རྒྱུད་ཀྱི་རྩ་རླུང་གཏུམ་མོའི་ལག་ལེན་
གསལ་བར་བཤད་པ་ནད་བརྒྱ་སེལ་བའི་སྨན་མཆོག་འཆི་མེད་ཚེ་ཡི་བདུད་རྩི་ཞེས་བྱ་བ་
བཞུགས།[1] – *Clear explanations on the daily practice of tsalung and tummo from the Mother Tantra, which is both an excellent medicine for healing hundreds of diseases and the essential elixir of immortality*, since Drubdra Khenpo's oral teachings include important additional clarifications and instructions vital for any practical application of these techniques.

This manual is significantly enriched by colour illustrations made by talented graphic artist Yungdrung Rabten whom we want to thank warmly for his wonderful work and dedication.

---

[1] Tib. Nyin re'i 'tsho ba'i nang du nye bar mkho ba'i gsang sngags ma rgyud kyi rtsa rlung gtum mo'i lag len gsal bar bshad pa nad brgya sel ba'i sman mchog 'chi med tshe yi bdud rtsi zhes bya ba bshugs.

As well as the series of photographs for each exercise included here, we have also prepared a video of Drubdra Khenpo demonstrating the movements as a further visual aid for those who want to practise these techniques. It was filmed in the North Pennines in November 2018 and can be viewed at www.yungdrungbon.co.uk/Multimedia.html

While these *tsalung* and *tummo* techniques are explained in detail here and can be practised safely, it is advisable to receive scriptural authorisation and further instructions from the master in order to further develop your practice and avoid common pitfalls.

We hope this book will be of benefit to many.

Dmitry Ermakov,
North Pennines, UK,
November 2018

Drubdra Khenpo Tsultrim Tenzin with FPYB's Carol Ermakova & Dmitry Ermakov, North Pennines, UK, November 2018.

2

About the Author

Khenpo Tsultrim Tenzin Rinpoche[2] was born in Yetha[3] in the Hor[4] region of East Tibet (Kham[5]), in 1968 to a Bönpo family of nomadic cattle herders. As a boy, he helped his family tend the sheep and yaks, and learnt reading and writing from his grandfather.

When he was nineteen, he entered the Lungkar[6] Monastery where he received teachings from *lamas* such as Uri Lama Nyima Lodrö[7] and Lopön Drangsong Yungdrung[8]. During this time, Tsultrim Tenzin completed the traditional preliminary practices and studied Tibetan grammar and poetry as well as various aspects of Bönpo[9] philosophy such as logic[10], *parchyin*[11], *wuma*[12], *dulwa*[13] and cosmology[14].

Tsultrim Tenzin served as *umze*[15], chant master, for three years in the Lungkar Monastery.

---

[2] Tib. Mkhan po Tshul khrims bstan 'dzin Rin po che / མཁན་པོ་ཚུལ་ཁྲིམས་བསྟན་འཛིན་ རིན་པོ་ཆེ།

[3] Tib. Ye tha / ཡེ་ཐ།

[4] Tib. Hor / ཧོར།

[5] Tib. Khams / ཁམས།

[6] Tib. Lung dkar / ལུང་དཀར།

[7] Tib. U ri Bla ma Nyi ma Blo gros / ཨུ་རི་བླ་མ་ཉི་མ་བློ་གྲོས།

[8] Tib. Slob dpon Drang srong g.yung drung / སློབ་དཔོན་དྲང་སྲོང་གཡུང་དྲུང་།

[9] Tib. bon po / བོན་པོ།

[10] Tib. tshad ma / ཚད་མ།

[11] Tib. phar phyin / ཕར་ཕྱིན། – Sanskr. pāramitā, a corpus of Sutra scriptures.

[12] Tib. dbu ma / དབུ་མ། – Sanskr. mādhyamaka, 'middle way' philosophy.

[13] Tib. 'dul ba / འདུལ་བ། – Sanskr. vinaya, rules of monastic conduct.

[14] Tib. mdzod / མཛོད། – Sanskr. abhidharma.

[15] Tib. dbu mzad / དབུ་མཛད།

Drubdra Khenpo Tsultrim Tenzin.

At the age of twenty-five, he moved to Menri[16] Monastery in Central Tibet where he studied with Pönlob Kalzang Nyima[17] from whom he received teachings on *Denö Dzö*[18] authored by Shardza Trashi Gyaltsen Rinpoche[19] (1859-1935) and the *A-Thri*[20] Bönpo Dzogchen manual. At this time he also gained the experiential

---

[16] Tib. Sman ri / སྨན་རི།

[17] Tib. Dpon slob Bskal bzang nyi ma / དཔོན་སློབ་སྐལ་བཟང་ཉི་མ།

[18] Tib. Sde snod mdzod / སྡེ་སྣོད་མཛོད།

[19] Tib. Shar rdza Bkra shis rgyal mtshan Rin po che / ཤར་རྫ་བཀྲ་ཤིས་རྒྱལ་མཚན་རིན་པོ་ཆེ།
– for biography, see Gyaltsen, Shardza Tashi. Commentary by Lopon Tenzin Namdak, Heart Drops of Dharmakaya: Dzogchen Practice of the Bön Tradition (Ithaca: Snow Lion Publications, 1993), pp. 17-29.

[20] Tib. A khrid / ཨ་ཁྲིད།

understanding of Great Perfection[21]. In 1993, Tsultrim Tenzin made the arduous journey to Triten Norbutse[22] Bönpo Monastery in Kathmandu, Nepal, to study intensively with his root Master Yongdzin Lopön Tenzin Namdak Rinpoche[23], under whose guidance he deepened his knowledge of Sutra, Tantra and Dzogchen[24]. He also learnt astrology[25], traditional Tibetan medicine[26], and Sanskrit.

While studying, Tsultrim Tenzin served as the monastery's chant master for six years, and as *gekhö*[27] (disciplinarian) for three years. After completing the 14-year study programme, he passed the Geshe[28] examination in 2001 and received his Geshe degree (roughly equivalent to Doctor of Philosophy).

The following year, in 2002, Tsultrim Tenzin was appointed, by Yongdzin Lopön Tenzin Namdak Rinpoche as Drubdra Khenpo[29] – Abbot of the Meditation School – in Triten Norbutse Monastery. Since then he has been teaching Dzogchen in the meditation school there as well as giving instructions on Sutra, Tantra, Dzogchen, astrology and mandala painting in the monastic dialectic school.

Alongside teaching, Khenpo Tsultrim Tenzin Rinpoche has been practising Dzogchen meditation and Magyu *tsalung*[30],

---

[21] Tib. rdzogs chen / རྫོགས་ཆེན།

[22] Tib. Khri brtan nor bu rtse / ཁྲི་བརྟན་ནོར་བུ་རྩེ།

[23] Tib. Yongs ‘dzin Slob dpon Bstan ‘dzin rnam dag Rin po che / ཡོངས་འཛིན་སློབ་དཔོན་བསྟན་འཛིན་རྣམ་དག་རིན་པོ་ཆེ།

[24] Tib. mdo sngags sems gsum / མདོ་སྔགས་སེམས་གསུམ།

[25] Tib. rtis / རྩིས།

[26] Tib. gso ba rig pa / གསོ་བ་རིག་པ།

[27] Tib. ge khod / གེ་ཁོད།

[28] Tib. dge bshes / དགེ་བཤེས།

[29] Tib. Sgrub grwa mkhan po / སྒྲུབ་གྲྭ་མཁན་པོ།

[30] Tib. rtsa rlung / རྩ་རླུང་། – practice of winds and channels.

thrulkhor[31] and *tummo*[32] for two hours every morning. He sometimes travels to Tibet, China, Japan, Europe and England to teach Dzogchen, Tantra and *tsalung*.

---

[31] Tib. 'phrul 'khor / འཕྲུལ་འཁོར། – literally 'magical wheel', 'machine', refers here to a series physical exercises.

[32] Tib. gtum mo / གཏུམ་མོ། – practice of 'inner heat'.

Introduction

A Brief History of the Magyu Lineage

Generally, we can talk about three types of Buddha, or three Buddha Bodies.[33] In Sanskrit they are known as *dharmakaya*, *sambhogakaya* and *nirmanakaya* and in Tibetan as *bönku, dzogku* and *trulku*[34]. The Magyu[35] or Mother Tantra was first taught by *dharmakaya* Buddha Kuntu Zangpo[36]. We can say that *dharmakaya* is Kuntu Zangpo and Kuntu Zangpo is *dharmakaya* – they are synonyms, so sometimes we use the name Bönku Kuntu Zangpo. Bönku Kuntu Zangpo transmitted this teaching to the *sambhogakaya* form, to Dzogku Kunzang Shenhla Wökar[37]. He appears as two different *sambhogakaya* forms, a peaceful one and a wrathful one. The peaceful form is known as Kunzang Khangying Karpo[38]. When we talk about the Five Buddha Families[39], Khangying Karpo is the Buddha in the centre of the mandala. The wrathful emanation is called Sangchog Tharthug Gyalpo[40] and has seven heads and sixteen arms. The Magyu teachings were transmitted from Bönku Kuntu Zangpo to Dzogku Khangying Karpo who transmitted to an emanation of Tönpa Shenrab[41] the *nirmanakaya* form called Trulku Chime Tsugphü[42]. Chime Tsugphü was born in the place of the

---

[33] Tib. sku gsum / སྐུ་གསུམ། – Sanskr. trikaya.

[34] Tib. bon sku, longs sku, sprul sku / བོན་སྐུ། ལོངས་སྐུ། སྤྲུལ་སྐུ།

[35] Tib. Ma rgyud / མ་རྒྱུད།

[36] Tib. Kun tu bzang po / ཀུན་ཏུ་བཟང་པོ།

[37] Tib. Rdzogs sku Kun bzang Gshen lha 'od dkar / རྫོགས་སྐུ་ཀུན་བཟང་གཤེན་ལྷ་འོད་དཀར།

[38] Tib. Kun bzang Mkha' 'gying dkar po / ཀུན་བཟང་མཁའ་འགྱིང་དཀར་པོ།

[39] Tib. rig lnga / རིགས་ལྔ།

[40] Tib. Gsang mchog Mthar thug rgyal po / གསང་མཆོག་མཐར་ཐུག་རྒྱལ་པོ།

[41] Tib. Ston pa Shen rab mi bo / སྟོན་པ་གཤེན་རབ་མི་བོ།

[42] Tib. Sprul sku 'Chi med gtsug phud / འཆི་མེད་གཙུག་ཕུད།

Thirty-Three Gods[43] and spoke *yungdrung hlake*[44], the Language of Swastika Gods (i.e. the language of Yungdrung Bön Buddhas). His father was called Thrulshen Nangden[45] and his mother was Zangza Ringtsün[46]. Thrulshen Nangden was an emanation of Khangying Karpo; he translated the Magyu tantras into Sanskrit[47] and taught them to both his son and his wife. So these two received Magyu teachings from him, and together with some dharma-friends such as Sangwa Düpa[48], Tagla Mebar[49] and so on, they attained Buddhahood. Sangwa Düpa translated Magyu into the language of Tagzig – *tagzig böngyike*[50] – and taught it in Tagzig.

Magyu passed from Chime Tsugphü to Gyalshen Milü Samleg[51] who was born in our world; some sources claim he lived somewhere near Kashmir, but this is not correct because the people where he lived spoke the Zhang Zhung language, *zhangzhung marke*[52], therefore that region must have been part of the Zhang Zhung Empire, somewhere to the West of Mount Tise[53] (Kailash).

---

[43] Tib. Sum chu rtsa gsum / སུམ་ཆུ་རྩ་གསུམ།

[44] Tib. G.yung drung lha skad / གཡུང་དྲུང་ལྷ་སྐད།

[45] Tib. 'Thrul gshen snang ldan / འཕྲུལ་གཤེན་སྣང་ལྡན།

[46] Tib. Bzang za ring btsun / བཟང་ཟ་རིང་བཙུན།

[47] Tib. sam skri ta skad / སཾ་ཀྲི་ཏའི་སྐད།

[48] Tib. Gsang ba 'dus pa / གསང་བ་འདུས་པ།

[49] Tib. Stag la me 'bar / སྟག་ལ་མེ་འབར།

[50] Tib. Stag gzig bon gyi skad / སྟག་གཟིག་བོན་གྱི་སྐད།

[51] Tib. Rgyal gshen Mi lus bsam legs / རྒྱལ་གཤེན་མི་ལུས་བསམ་ལེགས།

[52] Tib. zhang zhung smar skad / ཞང་ཞུང་སྨར་སྐད།

[53] Zzng. Ti se / ཏི་སེ།

8

Magyu tantric cycle with Sangchog Tharthug Gyalpo in the centre.

He was a king, and his palace was called Gyalkhar Bachö.[54] He received Magyu teachings from his master Hlashen Yongsu Dagpa[55], who was a student of Tönpa Shenrab (who had received these teachings from *sambhogakaya* Khangying Karpo). Hlashen Yongsu Dagpa was also the first in the lineage of the twenty-four masters of the *Zhang Zhung Nyengyud Dzogchen*[56]and he translated Magyu into the *zhangzhung marke* language.

Milü Samleg practised very well. He had many other teachers besides his main master Hlashen Yongsu Dagpa, from whom he also received many Dzogchen teachings. Milü Samleg became a Magyu *siddha*[57]. One day, some *khandro*[58] appeared to him and took him to the pure realm[59]. They took him to visit *khandro* Chyema Wötso[60]. Many *khandro* were gathered there, and they were all making offerings at a great Magyu *tsog*[61]. At that time Sangchog Tharthug Gyalpo was the *yidam*[62], Khangying Karpo was the *lama*, and Chyema Wötso was like the *umze*. So Milü Samleg suddenly found himself there, and he was very much surprised! Then Chyema Wötso gave him transmission, extremely fast, in one breath. So Milü Samleg received the complete transmission and then returned to earth. He practised *zhigyu*, *lamgyu* and *dregyu*[63] – the Tantra of the Base, the Tantra of the Path and the Tantra of the Fruit.

He practised the *zhigyu*, the Tantra of the Base, for fifty years, and had many students. Then he practised the Tantra of the

---

[54] Tib. Rgyal mkhar ba chod / རྒྱལ་མཁར་བ་ཆོད།

[55] Tib. Lha gshen Yongs su dag pa / ལྷ་གཤེན་ཡོངས་སུ་དག་པ།

[56] Tib. Zhang zhung snyan rgyud rdzogs chen / ཞང་ཞུང་སྙན་རྒྱུད་རྫོགས་ཆེན།

[57] Tib. grub thob / གྲུབ་ཐོབ།

[58] Tib. mkha' 'gro / མཁའ་འགྲོ།

[59] Tib. zhing khams / ཞིང་ཁམས།

[60] Tib. Kye ma 'od mtsho / ཀྱེ་མ་འོད་མཚོ།

[61] Tib. tshogs mchod / ཚོགས་མཆོད། – Sanskr. ganapuja.

[62] Tib. yi dam / ཡི་དམ།

[63] Tib. gzhi rgyud, lam rgyud, 'bras rgyud / གཞི་རྒྱུད། ལམ་རྒྱུད། འབྲས་རྒྱུད།

Path for another fifty years. Then he taught and practised the Tantra of the Fruit for another fifty years, so altogether he practised for a total of 150 years, and 5,500 of his students became *siddhas*. There were many *drubdra*[64] and g*omdra*[65] schools in his Gyalkhar Bachö palace.

His main student was called Phugpai Nangwa Dogchen[66]. He came from Central Zhang Zhung around Mount Tise and was a royal teacher of the first Tibetan King, Nyathri Tsenpo[67]. Phugpai Nangwa Dogchen received all the teachings from Milü Samleg. There are many lineage masters in this Magyu tradition. Nangwa Dogchen transmitted it to Barpai Anu Thragthag[68] from Middle Zhang Zhung. Then it went to Gopai Sene Gawu[69], who lived at the same time as the 8th King of Tibet, Drigum Tsenpo,[70] who destroyed a great many Bönpo teachings. Sene Gawu was from Outer Zhang Zhung, and he translated these teachings from the language of Zhang Zhung into Tibetan. In fact, we still find many Zhang Zhung passages in the Magyu texts. Because of the persecution of Yungdrung Bön unleashed by Drigum Tsenpo, Sene Gawu hid the Magyu texts in the ground.

---

[64] Tib. sgrub grwa / སྒྲུབ་གྲྭ། – *drubdra* and *gomdra* can generally be used as synonyms and are translated as 'meditation school' but in this case *drubdra* specifically means tantric meditation school.

[65] Tib. sgom grwa / སྒོམ་གྲྭ། – in this case Dzogchen meditation school.

[66] Tib. Phug pa'i Snang ba mdog can / ཕུག་པའི་སྣང་བ་མདོག་ཅན།

[67] Tib. Gnya' khri btsan po / གཉའ་ཁྲི་བཙན་པོ། – born 1136 BC according to the Bönpo Tentsi chronology (Tib. bstan rtsis) composed in 1842 by Menri Khenchen Nyima Tenzin (Tib. Sman ri Mkhan chen Nyi ma bstan 'dzin), the Abbot of Menri Monastery.

[68] Tib. Bar pa'i A nu thrag thag / བར་པའི་ཨ་ནུ་ཕྲག་ཐག།

[69] Tib. Sgo pa'i Sad ne ga'u / སྒོ་པའི་སད་ནེ་གའུ།

[70] Tib. Gri gum btsan po / གྲི་གུམ་བཙན་པོ། – born 710 BC according to the Bönpo Tentsi chronology.

Many, many years passed. In the twelfth century, over a thousand years later, a great *tertön*[71] treasure-revealer called Drubthob Guru Nöntse[72] discovered them. Actually, this man was a simple yak herder and a hunter, but he uncovered a lot of hidden texts, both Bönpo and Nyingma. So one day he was out herding his yaks when he came across the Tanag Dungphor[73] rock in Tsang[74], and that is where the Magyu texts were hidden. Although he found these teachings, he was a simple man who could read Tibetan but didn't really understand what was written in the texts he unearthed. So he gave them to a man called Nyaltön Zhönnubum[75] who read them very carefully and began copying them out. But before he had finished copying them all, the *tertön* suddenly came running up and called out: "*Khandro* are very powerful! Give me back the white scroll! Haven't you seen the five tigers in Tanag Dungphor?! Copied or not, give me back the texts!" So Nyaltön Zhönnubum gave the original texts back to Guru Nöntse who took them away and hid them again. To this day, nobody knows where they are.

The texts we have today are those Nyaltön Zhönnubum managed to copy back in the twelfth century[76]. And since that time, the lineage has never been broken. Yongdzin Tenzin Namdak Rinpoche is the current lineage holder, and he received all the Magyu teachings from Yongdzin Sanggye Tenzin[77] and the four initiations

---

[71] Tib. gter ston / གཏེར་སྟོན། – literally a 'treasure-revealer,' i.e. someone who discovers texts or ritual objects which have been hidden.

[72] Tib. Grub thob Gu ru rnon rtse / གྲུབ་ཐོབ་གུ་རུ་རྣོན་རྩེ། – born 1135 AD according to the Bönpo Tentsi chronology.

[73] Tib. Rta nag dung phor / རྟ་ནག་དུང་ཕོར།

[74] Tib. Gtsang / གཙང་།

[75] Tib. Myal ston Gzhon nu 'bum / མྱལ་སྟོན་གཞོན་ནུ་འབུམ།

[76] This account is according to Tib. Ma rgyud thugs rje nyi ma'i sgom 'drel nyi ma'i dkyil 'khor zhes bya ba'i dbu 'chad bzhugs so / མ་རྒྱུད་ཐུགས་རྗེ་ཉི་མའི་སྒོམ་འདྲེལ་ཉི་མའི་དཀྱིལ་འཁོར་ཞེས་བྱ་བའི་དབུ་འཆད་བཞུགས་སོ།།

[77] Tib. Yongs 'dzin Sangs rgya bstan 'dzin / ཡོངས་འཛིན་སངས་རྒྱ་བསྟན་འཛིན།

of Magyu from his master Shen Dzamling Rinpoche[78], a very great master who was not a monk; in fact, sometimes he traded horses. But he was a very great master. So – that is a brief story of the lineage.

Introduction to *tsalung*

Now I would like to tell you a little bit about *tsalung*. The Magyu teachings consist of both a root text and a commentary. The root text was transmitted by Kuntu Zangpo, while the commentary was written by Gyalshen Milü Samleg. There are very many chapters, and the chapter pertaining to *tsalung* is called *Thab lamchyer (Continuing along the Path of the Method)*. Teachings on *tsalung thrulkhor* are found in both the root text and the commentary, the Bönpo *Kangyur*[79] and *Tengyur*[80]. We can either practise according to the *Kangyur*, or according to the *Tengyur*, or we can practise these in combination. Yongdzin Rinpoche sometimes teaches from the root text, sometimes from the commentary, and sometimes he teaches a combination, because some aspects are clearer in one text or the other.

It is very important for practitioners to learn and practise *tsalung*. It can greatly benefit your meditation by helping your mind become more stable. If your mind is stable, you can meditate more easily. If your mind is not stable, you can't meditate properly. Why not? Because 'meditation' means focussing on something one-pointedly. If you have a lot of thoughts and your mind is always chasing after them, then this causes obstacles for your meditation. We talk about three main obstacles:

- Strengthlessness, *jingwa*[81]

---

[78] Tib. Gshen 'Dzam gling Rin po che / གཤེན་འཛམ་གླིང་རིན་པོ་ཆེ།

[79] Tib. Bka' 'gyur / བཀའ་འགྱུར། – a compendium of the Words of the Buddha.

[80] Tib. Brtan 'gyur / བརྟེན་འགྱུར། – a compendium of the commentaries of the realised Masters.

[81] Tib. bying ba / བྱིང་བ།

- Agitation, *göpa*[82]
- Dullness, *mugpa*[83]

If you practise *tsalung* properly then these obstacles disappear automatically; there is no place, no space, for any of these three conditions to arise. *Tsalung* helps make your mind stable, and when your mind is stable, there is no place for agitation and so on to arise, so they naturally subside.

Tsalung in the context of Bönpo Tantra

Strictly speaking, *tsalung* belongs to Tantra teachings. There are two stages in Tantra, the generation stage, *chyerim*[84], and the completion stage, *dzogrim*[85] and *tsalung* belongs to the latter. Tantric practitioners should first practise *chyerim*, then *dzogrim*. The final result is *gyulü*[86], the illusory body, and *detong yeshe*[87], the primordial wisdom of inseparable bliss and emptiness. If you practise *chyerim* well, the ultimate result appears. For a tantric practitioner, this means s/he must practise the visualisation of their *yidam* with absolute concentration. Sometimes they can visualise the *yidam* as very tiny and minute, the size of a sesame seed. Or sometimes they can visualise the *yidam* as big as Mount Meru. Once you have practised for a long time and become very familiar with this, you can choose how you do the visualisation. That means that even if you visualise the whole *mandala* in miniature, small enough to fit on your thumbnail, with all the *yidams* and retinue like tiny sesame seeds, still everything is extremely clear and distinct, even the *yidams'* eyes are very bright. That is the ultimate goal of *chyerim*.

---

[82] Tib. rgod pa / རྒོད་པ།

[83] Tib. smug pa / སྨུག་པ།

[84] Tib. bskyed rim / བསྐྱེད་རིམ།

[85] Tib. rdzogs rim / རྫོགས་རིམ།

[86] Tib. sgyu lus / སྒྱུ་ལུས།

[87] Tib. bde strong ye shes / བདེ་སྟོང་ཡེ་ཤེས.

But it is not enough. A tantric practitioner also needs to add the experience of *detong yeshe,* the primordial wisdom of inseparable bliss and emptiness. There are special methods for developing this. First of all, you should remain in your Natural State[88] and then apply special methods. If you practise properly, bliss and emptiness will arise and finally unite inseparably – bliss is emptiness, emptiness is bliss, and these two are united with wisdom. This bliss arises from your Natural State, it is not a sensation of ordinary bliss.

Finally, from this, you make the *yidam* body in your heart. So, if you practise *chyerim* and *dzogrim* perfectly, you create the illusory body. That is the union or manifestation of your ordinary subtle mind, *sem*[89], and *lung*[90], wind or energy. We can say that in this case, the *yidam*'s body is made of *lung* and *sem* and together this *sem* and *lung* make *gyulü*, and finally you become a new form of the *yidam.*

But still this is not enough. You need to combine this with *detong yeshe.* So we can say that the *detong yeshe* is like the *yidam's* mind and *gyulü* is the *yidam*'s body and these two together are like a new entity. This is the real *yidam* which you created yourself. If you don't practise *chyerim* and *dzogrim* but visualise the *yidam* from time to time, this is all just your own imagination. *Gyulü* is the real *yidam.* So in this case we can say you have two bodies, your own body with your own mind, but also the *yidam* body with *detong yeshe.* If you advance to this stage, then sometimes when you take your *yidam*'s body, your ordinary body is sort of hidden inside, it disappears, and ordinary people can't see you. Sometimes you take your ordinary form and then they can see your body. But you still have to practise *dzogrim* more and more: *gyulü* plus *detong yeshe* – that is the real *dzogrim* practice.

---

[88] Tib. gnas lugs, sems nyid / གནས་ལུགས། སེམས་ཉིད།

[89] Tib sems / སེམས།

[90] Tib. rlung / རླུང་།

You also need to purify this *yidam*'s body. Why? Because it is 'made' of your ordinary mind (your subtle mind, *sem*) and *lung*, so it is called *madagpai gyulü*[91], an impure illusory body. Thus you should continue practising until finally your ordinary subtle mind and *lung* completely disappear and the quality of both your mind and your body becomes as *detong yeshe*. That is called *dagpai gyulü*[92], pure illusory body. In this case, 'impure' means still connected with ordinary mind and *lung*, but at this final stage even the subtle mind and *lung* are purified through practice, so you have realised *dagpai gyulü*. Then we can say you have become the real *yidam*, a tantric Buddha. This *tsalung* can be applied as a practice or method for developing *detong yeshe*, in *dzogrim*.

Tsalung in the context of Dzogchen

But if we are not tantric practitioners, we don't need to practise *chyerim* and *dzogrim*; if we are *dzogchenpas*[93] our main practice is remaining in the Natural State. So in this case we can use this practice of *tsalung* as a method to pacify the obstacles of agitation, dullness and strengthlessness that arise and disturb our meditation. Practising this *tsalung* perfectly and completely can relax you deeply. Your body becomes smooth, without any tensions, and your mind calms down, too. When your body and mind are both relaxed, you can remain in the Natural State; your Natural State or awareness[94] arise very clearly.

How can you check whether this is real Dzogchen meditation? How can you correct your meditation if something is not right? You can use this *tsalung* method and that will give you experience of very clear, strong meditation, so you can correct it this way.

---

[91] Tib. ma dag pa'i sgyu lus / མ་དག་པའི་སྒྱུ་ལུས།

[92] Tib. dag pa'i sgyu lus / དག་པའི་སྒྱུ་ལུས།

[93] Tib. rdzogs chen pa / རྫོགས་ཆེན་པ། – a practitioner of Dzogchen.

[94] Tib. rig pa / རིག་པ།

This applies to all types of meditation, not just when you remain in the Natural State; if you practise Guru Yoga[95] or a *yidam* and your practice becomes a little dull or something, you can do this *tsalung* and afterwards your meditation will be very clear and strong. Then you can practise whatever you like – Guru Yoga, a *yidam*, *bodhichitta*, whatever you like – and it will be clear because now your mind is much more stable, much clearer. All types of meditation work with the mind more than with the body or speech, so according to Dzogchen, this *tsalung* is like medicine – it is not the main practice, but everybody needs it.

A brief explanation of *tsalung*, *thrulkhor*, *thigle* and *tummo*

Tsa

Tsa means 'channel.' In general, there are many *tsa* or channels in our body. We say there are around 21,000 different channels – in fact, we can say they are countless. There are two types of channels: *netsa*[96] the channels which naturally abide in our body; and *gomtsa*[97], the meditation channels, the ones we visualise. There are three main *gomtsa*: right, left and central[98].

As for the *netsa*, there are a great many, but we can talk of two main categories:
- *Nyonmongpai tsa*[99] through which winds of emotions circulate;
- *Yeshekyi tsa*[100], or wisdom channels through which wisdom winds circulate.

---

[95] Tib. bla ma'i rnal 'byor / བླ་མའི་རྣལ་འབྱོར།

[96] Tib. gnas rtsa / གནས་རྩ།

[97] Tib. sgom rtsa / སྒོམ་རྩ།

[98] Tib. g.yas dkar, g.yon dmar, dbu mthing / གཡས་དཀར། གཡོན་དམར། དབུ་མཐིང་།

[99] Tib. nyon mongs pa'i rtsa / ཉོན་མོངས་པའི་རྩ།

[100] Tib. ye shes kyi rtsa / ཡེ་ཤེས་ཀྱི་རྩ།

There are also many kinds of *lung* – breath or wind – in our body such as the wisdom-bliss wind *yeshekyi delung*[101],and the rough wind of emotions *nyonmongpai tsublung*[102] and they all move through the channels; if there were no channels, there would be no space for the winds to move.

As for the three main channels (the central, right and left channels) the right white channel is for the white *thigle*[103], which represents vital male essence which is white, while the red channel is for *rakta*[104], the red *thigle*, which represents red vital female essence. We can say that *dongpo sum*[105], the three main channels, are like the trunk of a tree, and the chakras are like branches, while the petals are like leaves.

The central channel (*wuma*) is blue on the outside and pink inside and is for the Empty aspect of Nature; the right channel is white, for the Clarity aspect of Nature; the left channel is red, for the Bliss aspect of Nature. As I said before, *detong yeshe* has three qualities – bliss, emptiness and wisdom or clarity – so these three channels represent *detong yeshe*. These three aspects are very important for anyone who practises *detong yeshe* since you cannot have a full experience of it without working with these three main channels.

Chakras

As for the chakras, according to Magyu, there are five: crown chakra of the great bliss, throat chakra of enjoyment, heart chakra of the Nature of phenomenal existence, navel chakra of emanation, and

---

[101] Tib. ye shes kyi bde rlung / ཡེ་ཤེས་ཀྱི་བདེ་རླུང་།

[102] Tib. nyon mongs pa'i rtsub rlung / ཉོན་མོངས་པའི་རྩུབ་རླུང་།

[103] Tib. thig le / ཐིག་ལེ།

[104] Tib. rak ta / རཀྟ།

[105] Tib. sdong po gsum / སྡོང་པོ་གསུམ།

18

secret chakra of method and wisdom[106], although some texts speak of six.

The chakras have petals around them, and the number of petals varies from text to text, too. For instance, some texts mention four petals in the crown chakra, while others talk of twelve and so on. According to Magyu, the crown chakra has 32 petals and the 32 great *khandro* of immeasurable compassion[107] abide on them spontaneously, naturally. When you practise *chyerim* you visualise the 32 *khandro* on the petals of this chakra, but in fact, they already abide there spontaneously.

The throat chakra has 16 petals and the 16 incessant great mother *khandro*[108] abide there.

The twelve petals in the heart chakra stand for the eight wrathful *khandro* manifestations of compassion[109], and the four Female Buddhas of great bliss[110]. You can visualise them here, but they abide there spontaneously. You visualise them when you do *chyerim*, but when you achieve Buddhahood, these *khandro* appear from the chakras spontaneously.

The navel chakra has 64 petals which correspond to 64 goddesses[111]. 60 are offering *khandro* and 4 *khandro* are holding implements[112]: one holds a hook; one holds a lasso; one holds a

---

[106] Tib. spyi bob de chen gyi 'khor lo, mgrin pa longs spyod kyi 'khor lo, thugs kha bon nyid kyi 'khor lo, lte sprul pa'i 'khor lo, gsang gnas thabs shes kyi 'khor lo / སྤྱི་བོ་བདེ་ཆེན་གྱི་འཁོར་ལོ། མགྲིན་པ་ལོངས་སྤྱོད་ཀྱི་འཁོར་ལོ། ཐུགས་ཁ་བོན་ཉིད་ཀྱི་འཁོར་ལོ། ལྟེ་བ་སྤྲུལ་པའི་འཁོར་ལོ། གསང་གནས་ཐབས་ཤེས་ཀྱི་འཁོར་ལོ།

[107] Tib. tshad med yum chen so gnyis / ཚད་མེད་ཡུམ་ཆེན་སོ་གཉིས།

[108] Tib. rgyun med yum chen bcu drug / རྒྱུན་མེད་ཡུམ་ཆེན་བཅུ་དྲུག

[109] Tib. thugs rje rol pa'i khro mo brgyad / ཐུགས་རྗེ་རོལ་པའི་ཁྲོ་མོ་བརྒྱད།

[110] Tib. bde chen sangs rgyas yum bzhi / བདེ་ཆེན་སངས་རྒྱས་ཡུམ་བཞི།

[111] Tib. 'dod yon lha mo drug bcu rtsa bzi / འདོད་ཡོན་ལྷ་མོ་དྲུག་བཅུ་རྩ་བཞི།

[112] Tib. go cha ma bzhi / གོ་ཆ་མ་བཞི།

shang and one holds shackles[113]. In Tantra, we talk about *yeshe sempa*[114] and *damtsig sempa*[115], or the *samaya* deity and the wisdom deity. For instance, if I practise Magyu Tantra, I visualise myself as Sangchog Tharthug Gyalpo. In this instance, I am Sangchog Tharthug Gyalpo, my mind is Sangchog Tharthug Gyalpo, there is no difference between the two. This is *damtsig sempa*. Sometimes we visualise the *mandala* together with the many attributes we put on the *mandala* such as a *bumpa*[116] etc. At that time we visualise many deities there, and these are all *damtsig sempa*. But this is not enough. We need to invite the wisdom deities, *yeshe sempa*, from the pure realm, and it is two *khandro* out of these four who invite the wisdom deities: the Hook-holder and Lasso-holder invite the wisdom deities – they 'catch' them if you like – and bring them down so the wisdom deities appear before the practitioner. Then the Bell-holder *khandro* makes extensive offerings to the wisdom deities. The wisdom deities then dissolve into the practitioner's visualisation, the *damtsig sempa*, and these two become inseparable, non-dual. The Chain-holder 'binds' them so they are integrated together inseparably until the conclusion of the *sadhana*. This is the meaning of the symbols these four *khandro* hold in their hands.

The chakra in the secret place[117] has four petals and they correspond to the four door-keeper *khandro*[118] who guard the inner doors[119] of the *mandala*. Actually, there are many doors into the

---

[113] Tib. myur mgyogs glog 'gyu ma, thugs rje sprin dpung ma, byin rlabs char pa ma, mi 'gyur g.yung drung ma / སྱུར་མགྱོགས་གློག་འགྱུ་མ། ཐུགས་རྗེ་སྤྲིན་དཔུང་ མ། བྱིན་རླབས་ཆར་པ་མ། མི་འགྱུར་གཡུང་དྲུང་མ།

[114] Tib. ye shes sems dpa' / ཡེ་ཤེས་སེམས་དཔའ།

[115] Tib. dam tshig sems dpa' / དམ་ཚིག་སེམས་དཔའ།

[116] Tib. bum pa / བུམ་པ།

[117] This roughly corresponds to the area four fingers below the navel.

[118] Tib. sgo ma bzhi / སྒོ་མ་བཞི།

[119] Tib. nang sgo / ནང་སྒོ།

Magyu *mandala*, 16 in total, but these *khandro* guard the four inner doors.

So this is a brief explanation of why each chakra has a certain number of petals.

But why are there five chakras in the Magyu system, not six? In the crown chakra we visualise Bönku Kuntu Zangpo.
In the throat chakra – Khangying Karpo.
In the heart chakra – Sangchog Tharthug Gyalpo.
In the navel chakra – Chime Tsugphü
In the secret chakra – Zangza Ringtsün.
Hence five chakras.

Lung

Lung means wind. As we have seen, the channels or *tsa* are hollow, and act as passageways; winds or *lung* come and go in some, blood passes through others, and *thigles* travel through still others. There are many different winds, and although we generally speak of nine, we can categorise them into two main groups: *yeshekyi delung* and *nyonmongpai tselung*. The former, the wisdom bliss wind, circulates through the red left channel while the latter, the wind of afflicting emotions, circulates through the white right channel.

Then there are five *lungs* we work with during our *tsalung* practice, the five root winds:

Upward-moving wind	**Earth element**	**Yellow**
Life-supporting wind	**Space element**	**White**
Fire-equalising wind	Fire element	Red
All-pervading wind	**Wind element**	**Green**
Downward-moving wind[120]	Water element	Blue

---

[120] Tib. gyen rgyu'i rlung, srog 'dzin gyi rlung, me mnyam gyi rlung, khyab byed kyi rlung, thur sel gyi rlung / གྱེན་རྒྱུའི་རླུང་། སྲོག་འཛིན་གྱི་རླུང་། མེ་མཉམ་གྱི་རླུང་། ཁྱབ་བྱེད་ཀྱི་རླུང་། ཐུར་སེལ་གྱི་རླུང་།

The upward-moving wind resides in the area between the neck to the brain and is connected to the nose.

The life-supporting wind resides in the heart and lungs.

The fire-equalising wind resides in the stomach and intestines.

The all-pervading wind spreads from the throat chakra throughout the whole body but resides particularly in the limbs.

The downward-moving wind resides in the secret chakra, in the so-called lower doors, below the intestine.

Each one has a symbol[121]. These five root winds are extremely important, they govern all the functions of our body, whatever we do.

There are many different *lungs* we could talk about, but if you understand these seven, that is sufficient for our purposes here.

Thrulkhor

Thrulkhor means 'working with the body.' For instance, in The Key Point of the *Lung* Practice with Four Aspects, the first *thrulkhor* movements work with the upward-moving wind and our neck. We move other parts of our body in the subsequent *thrulkhor,* so we could say that 'thrulkhor' means 'exercise'.

Thigle

To put it simply, we can say that 'thigle' means 'vital essence' as we discussed earlier although in other contexts it can refer to the Natural State. In the Magyu teachings, semen and menstrual blood are referred to as *thigles*, or as male and female vital essences. It is very important for those who practise *detong yeshe* to work with these two *thigles*. They are also the seed of life, the cause for birth. In the *tummo* breathing taught here, we visualise petals and a triangle of fire below the *khandro*. This is very important since in this case, the petals are the antidote to the womb, to taking another rebirth; overall, *chyerim* practice is the antidote to death, *bardo*[122] and

---

[121] See page 30 below.

[122] Tib. bar do / བར་དོ།

rebirth. There are two reasons why we visualise these petals: firstly, they symbolise purifying the mother's womb, the seat of birth, and in this way we purify the negativity of birth which brings us into *samsara*. Secondly, the flower cushion represents Buddha, or *sanggye*[123] in Tibetan, which means 'totally purified' from the very beginning.

The sun disc is the antidote to the mother's menstrual blood and at the same time, it also represents Buddha's wisdom.

Similarly, according to *chyerim*, the moon disc represents the antidote to the father's seed, semen, but it also represents the methods taught by Buddha – Buddha needed very powerful methods to lead sentient beings out of *samsara*.

There are many other kinds of *thigle* besides these two vital essences, such as *rigpai thigle, semnyi thigle, yenyi thigle, samten thigle*[124] which refer to the Natural State:

Rigpai thigle – thigle of Awareness;
Semnyi thigle – thigle of the Nature of Mind;
Yenyi thigle – thigle of Primordial Nature;
Samten thigle – thigle of concentrating in the Natural State without agitation.

Tummo

I have already mentioned the triangle of fire in the secret chakra. In Magyu, we sometimes visualise the *khandro* representing protection. Or sometimes we simply visualise the small pyramid of fire.

The word *tummo*[125] just means 'wrathful'; 'tum' means 'wrathful'. In this case, the *khandro* is not wrathful, it is the fire

---

[123] Tib. sangs rgyas / སངས་རྒྱས།

[124] Tib. rig pa'i thig le, sems nyid, ye nyid thig le, bsam gtan thig le / རིག་པའི་ ཐིག་ལེ། སེམས་ཉིད་ཐིག་ལེ། ཡེ་ཉིད་ཐིག་ལེ། བསམ་གཏན་ཐིག་ལེ།

[125] Tib. gtum mo / གཏུམ་མོ།

which is blazing vigorously. And 'mo' here refers to blood; the suffix 'mo' usually denotes female.

As we saw earlier, for tantric practitioners, the purpose of practising *tummo* is twofold:

Firstly, since we humans have both body and mind, we need to realise pure mind and pure body. Through practising *tummo* we achieve both *gyulü* and *detong yeshe*.

Secondly, practising *tummo* is very beneficial for our health. Because when your inner heat is stronger, any disease or imbalance you have can be cured if you practise well.

And of course, the benefits for meditation are enormous.

Health benefits of *tsalung*

This *tsalung* helps your health, of course. If you already have some health problem, some disease, and you practise this method of *tsalung thrulkhor* properly then it can help ease your condition and maybe eventually it will disappear. Why? How does this work?

Practising *tsalung* returns energy to your inner organs, to your liver, heart, lungs, kidney, spleen, stomach etc, so as you practise more and more, these organs are revitalised. This is much more effective than taking vitamins! For example, if you have some digestive problem, practising the breathing and visualisation connected with the navel chakra will be of great benefit.

According to our teachings, there are five winds or energies (*lung*) that reside in our body. The upward-moving wind resides in the throat chakra; the life-supporting wind resides in the heart chakra; the fire-equalising wind resides in the stomach or navel chakra; the downward-moving wind resides in the secret chakra, and the all-pervading wind resides in the limbs. Each of the *tsalung* exercises focusses on one of these winds or energies. They are extremely important for our bodies. If for instance something is wrong with our upward-moving wind, we might have problems with our brain or not be able to speak properly. If the life-supporting wind is weak, you can have heart trouble and your lifespan may decrease. If your fire-equalising wind doesn't function properly then your

24

stomach doesn't work well, whereas if your downward-moving wind is weak, you will have difficulties urinating, defecating etc. Similarly, if the all-pervading wind is out of balance, you many have problems with your limbs, stiffness or arthritis etc. When all your five winds or energies are harmoniously balanced, then automatically your body will be healthy. This *tsalung* practice is very effective in fortifying and strengthening the five winds, and that in turn revitalises the respective organs. For example, if your life-supporting energy is strong, your heart will be strong, too. When your fire-equalising wind is in good condition, it helps your stomach but also your liver, kidneys and spleen because they are all more-or-less at the same level in your body, the level of your navel chakra, so they are all affected when you do this exercise.

This practice is of great benefit for both health and spiritual practice.

Daily Magyu *tsalung* and *tummo* practice

according to the
"Clear explanations on the daily practice of tsalung and tummo
from the Mother Tantra, which is both an excellent medicine
for healing hundreds of diseases
and the essential elixir of immortality"

ཉིན་རེའི་འཚོ་བའི་ནད་དུ་ཉེ་བར་མཁོ་བའི་གསང་སྔགས་མ་རྒྱུད་ཀྱི་རྩ་རླུང་གཏུམ་མོའི་
ལག་ལེན་གསལ་བར་བཤད་པ་ནད་བརྒྱ་སེལ་བའི་སྨན་མཆོག་
འཆི་མེད་ཚེ་ཡི་བདུད་རྩི་ཞེས་བྱ་བ་བཞུགས།

by Drubdra Khenpo Tsultrim Tenzin

Nine-Pointed Body Posture

1. The Key Point of the Nine-Pointed Body Posture:

དང་པོ་བཅའ་བ་ལུས་ཀྱི་གནད།

1. Sit straight up.
2. Cross your legs in the half or full lotus position.
3. Keep your spine straight.
4. Place your hands together, palms upwards, left over right below the navel in the *mudra*[126] of equipoise, with the thumb of each hand resting on the base of the respective ring finger.
5. Your neck should be 'tied like a knot' (i.e. your chin should be tucked in slightly so your neck is 'closed').
6. Let your eyes gaze in front of you, at the level of your nose[127].
7. Your shoulders should be slightly raised, with your elbows out, like Garuda's [128] wings.
8. Keep your mind and body alert neither slack nor tense.
9. Meditation belt; if you tend to slip out of the posture, you can use a meditation belt around your knees and the small of your back to hold the position tightly. This will automatically raise your shoulders slightly.

Mudra of equipoise.

---

[126] Tib. phyag rgya / ཕྱག་རྒྱ།
[127] I.e. a point an arm's length in front of you at the level of the tip of your nose. During visualization the eyes can be closed.
[128] Tib. khyung / ཁྱུང་། – mythical bird and a tantric *yidam*.

Tsalung Tummo posture using a meditation belt.

2. The Key Point of the Visualisation of the Channels
གཉིས་པ་བསྐྱེད་པ་རྩ་ཡི་གནད།

The central channel is blue outside and pink inside. It rises from the secret place and at its base it is the width of a stick of bamboo. As it rises, it gradually widens until it is the size of the circle you make with your index finger and thumb.

It resembles a *ragdung*[129] long trumpet, standing on end, open at the top.

Diameter of the central channel at the top.

The left and right channels are hollow, very clean, very straight and are the width of an arrow. They connect with the central channel in the secret place and rise straight up inside your torso.

The left channel is red. The right channel is white.

They cross over at the back of your head (left over right), then come up and round and cross over again at your forehead with the left channel on top, so the right channel reaches the right nostril and the left channel reaches the left nostril.

All three channels are very subtle. Their walls are as fine as a petal.

---

[129] Tib. rag dung / རག་དུང་།

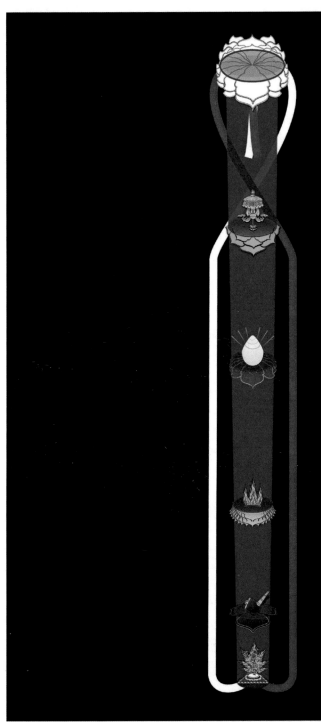

Channels and chakras according to Magyu *tummo* and *tsalung*.

3. The Key Point of Visualising the Winds

གསུམ་པ་བསྒོམ་པ་རླུང་གི་གནད།

Chakras

Visualise the five chakras: crown, throat, heart, navel, secret chakra (two parts). Each chakra has a number of petals outside and a symbol in the centre representing the respective wind:

1. Crown chakra	32 white petals
2. Throat chakra	16 green petals
3. Heart chakra	12 red petals
4. Navel chakra	64 yellow petals
5 a. Secret chakra **5 b. Secret chakra**	4 blue petals a red triangle

Visualise this as clearly as possible.

Crown chakra.

Throat chakra.

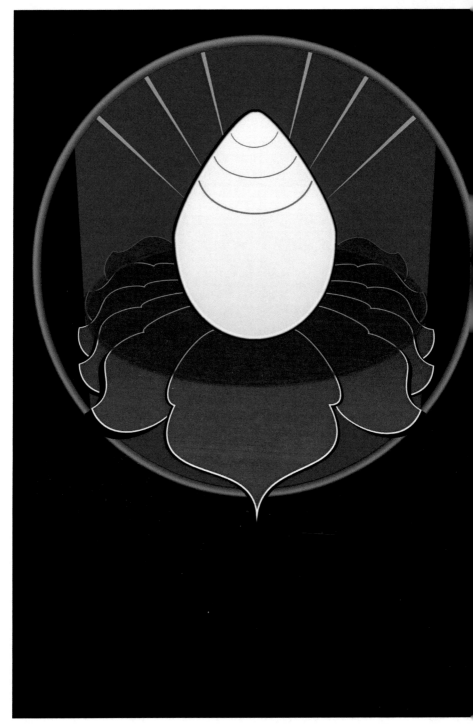

Heart chakra.

Navel chakra.

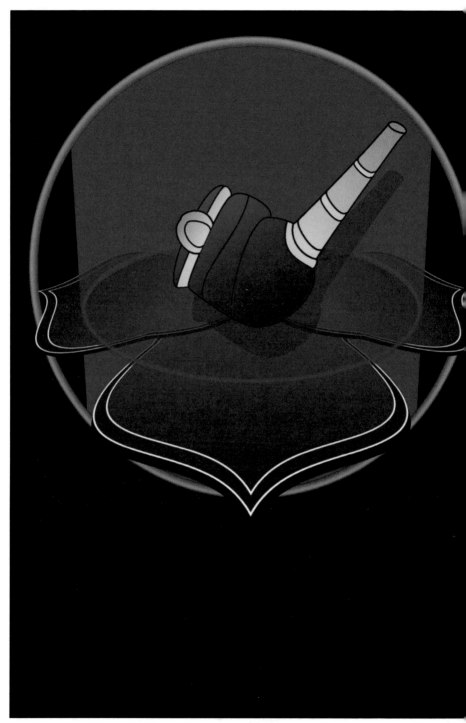

Secret chakra (a).

Secret chakra (b).

CROWN CHAKRA	no symbol
THROAT CHAKRA	yellow umbrella symbolising the upward-moving wind
HEART CHAKRA	white *norbu*[130], a wish-fulfilling jewel symbolising the life-supporting wind
NAVEL CHAKRA	three-flamed fire symbolising the fire-equalising wind
WHOLE BODY	visualise a green colour representing the all-pervading wind which spreads throughout your whole body, like the rays of the sun. Your torso is a paler green, filled with pale green light, while your limbs are darker green
SECRET CHAKRA (a) SECRET CHAKRA (b)	blue bellows symbolising the downward-moving wind. The secret chakra has two parts; the bellows are in the upper part while the triangle of fire on which the *khandro* stands is in the lower part

The chakras are inside the central channel, the petals protrude through the wall of the central channel on the outside, horizontally,

---

[130] Tib. nor bu / ནོར་བུ།

while the yellow umbrella, white *norbu*, three-flamed fire and blue bellows and *khandro* are each in the centre of their respective chakra.

Visualise this very well.

First check the body posture, then visualise the channels, then the chakras, with their petals, then visualise the symbols of the five winds. Visualise these one by one.

Winds

These five winds work in the body; they are working whenever we do anything – eating, sleeping and so on. We do many things automatically – inhaling, exhaling, walking etc. – so these five winds are always working. If something is wrong with them, you have a problem.

The upward-moving wind governs your neck, talking, the movement of the tongue, and the sense of taste; this is all controlled by the upward-moving wind.

The life-supporting wind resides in the heart chakra and it controls many things, including mental processes. If it is working well, then you can have a long life. If it is out of balance, then you may have a heart problem, or a short life. This wind affects all your organs, because the channels to the main organs (heart, kidneys, lungs, liver and spleen) spread out from the heart chakra so if your life-supporting wind is in perfect condition, then all your organs are healthy and your channels function smoothly. It is very easy to get problems in the liver or any other organ if something is amiss with this wind.

The fire-equalising wind resides in the navel chakra. It mainly governs digestion. Since the liver is closely connected with the stomach, if your digestive system is working very well, then your liver has no problem, you have no problem with your lower doors

39

and so on. If your digestion is poor, then you may have many problems with your lower doors, your stomach, your liver etc.

The all-pervading wind is spread throughout your whole body, inside the organs and outside. It spreads like the rays of the sun. It governs the function of your limbs. If this wind is balanced, then your knees, legs, hands, fingers and so on are all fine. You may experience joint pain or trouble if this wind is out of balance.

The downward-moving wind resides in the secret place. If there is something wrong with it, then your lower doors do not function properly and it is difficult to pass urine or stools; there may be many problems.

UPWARD-MOVING WIND	Governs neck, talking, movement of the tongue, sense of taste
LIFE-SUPPORTING WIND	Controls mental processes, duration of life and the heart as well as kidneys, lungs, liver & spleen
FIRE-EQUALISING WIND	Mainly governs digestion, controls stomach, liver, intestines etc.
ALL-PERVADING WIND	Spreads throughout the body. Controls movement of limbs: arms, legs, joints, fingers etc.
DOWNWARD-MOVING WIND	Controls lower doors, function of elimination

4. The Key Point of Nine Purification Breathings

བཞི་པ་དུག་རླུང་འབུད་པ།

When your visualisation is very clear, do the nine purification breathings.

Place your thumbs at the base of your ring fingers.
Leaving your right hand in your lap, close your right nostril with the ring finger of your left hand and inhale through your left nostril, quite slowly.

Then close your left nostril with the ring finger of your left hand, and exhale through your right nostril, starting gently and ending quite strongly. As you exhale, imagine the four negativities of: wind disease, disturbances sent by male spirits, anger and past karma are purified.

Repeat this three times.

Then place your left hand in your lap, close your left nostril with the ring finger of your right hand and inhale through your right nostril, quite slowly.

Then close your right nostril with the ring finger of your right hand, and exhale through your left nostril, starting gently and ending quite strongly. As you exhale, imagine the four negativities of: bile disease, disturbances sent by female spirits, desire and future karma are purified.

Repeat this three times.

With both hands in your lap in the pose of equanimity, inhale through both nostrils so the breath flows through both side channels and enters the central channel at the junction of the channels, four fingers below your navel. Then exhale strongly through both nostrils, visualising the wind is exhaled through the central channel, through the opening at the crown of your head. Imagine the four negativities of: phlegm, disturbances sent by *nagas*[131], ignorance and present karma are purified.

Repeat this three times.

Some texts, such as *Kusum Rangshar*[132], describe the exhalations with colours. However, no colours are mentioned in the Magyu, or the *Zhang Zhung Nyengyu*. Nevertheless, you can use colours if you like.

Inhaling (left side).

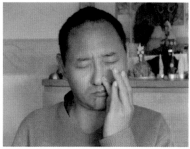

Exhaling (right side).

Inhaling (right side).

Exhaling (left side).

Exhaling (both nostrils, central channel).

---

[131] Tib. klu / ཀླུ། – water spirits.

[132] Tib. Sku gsum rang shar / སྐུ་གསུམ་རང་ཤར།

5. The Key Point of the Lung Practice with Four Aspects

ཕ་པ་རླུང་སྦྱོར་ཡན་ལག་བཞི་ལ་བསྐབ་པ།

Now we practise the Lung Practice with Four Aspects: inhaling, holding, re-inhaling, exhaling.

Inhale slowly and smoothly through both nostrils. Visualise the wind or breath coming through the side channels into the central channel and slowly filling up the central channel, rising through the secret chakra, the navel chakra, the heart chakra, and the throat chakra right up to the crown chakra.

Hold your breath.

The all-pervading wind spreads throughout your body and limbs.

The longer you hold your breath, the more the benefit. Re-inhale to top up at least three times. If you can re-inhale more than three times, your body will become hotter and hotter, and the benefit will be greater. Add a few more seconds to the retention each day as you train.

Focus on all five winds at once.

When you are ready, exhale slowly and strongly through both nostrils.

When you exhale very strongly at the end of this long exhalation, all the bone marrow between your vertebrae shakes, and that is very beneficial.

Leave the lower doors in the normal way. Since it is difficult for beginners to close them, some problems may arise if you try to do so. If you are familiar with this practice, then you can close your lower doors. In my opinion, during *tsalung*, *thrulkhor* and *tummo* practice, it is important to settle into the body posture very well, and then relax. Just relax. Don't move, don't do anything. There is no need to pull in the stomach or close the lower doors, nothing. Just do this Lung Practice with Four Aspects.

When you hold the breath, don't let your mind be distracted. Focus on the winds in the central channel; that is most important.

This is the Lung Practice with Four Aspects.

This is the foundation of *tsalung* practice; you need this for any *tsalung* or *tummo* practice.

If you are doing a retreat with a view to developing this *lung* practice, then you can repeat this section many times. Maybe for a whole day, repeating it 3, 5, 7, 9, etc. up to 21 times. I usually practise it once, then move on.

Posture for The Key Point of the Lung Practice with Four Aspects.

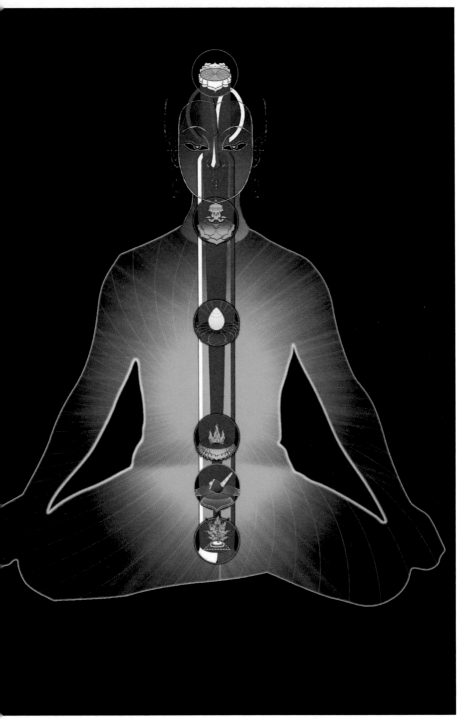

Visualisation for The Key Point of the Lung Practice with Four Aspects.

6. The Key Point of the Practice of the Five Winds

དྲག་པ་ཚ་བའི་རླུང་ཐམས་ལུས་སྟོང་གི་བདེ་དྲོད་སྦར་བ།

i) Upward-moving Wind

Inhale slowly and smoothly through both nostrils.

Focus on the wind entering the central channel through the two side channels. It mainly dissolves in the throat chakra, in the petals. Then focus mostly on the yellow umbrella.

Hold your breath.

When you are ready, re-inhale, then:

Rotate your head to the right, five times.

Rotate your head to the left, five times.

Nod your head forcefully but slowly backwards and forwards, five times.

Remain relaxed and focus on the yellow umbrella as you do this.

When you exhale, sound either: HEE HEENG (the sound which pleases the *lama*); HU HUNG (the sound which makes the *yidam* happy) or HUNG SHRI[133] (the sound which calls the *khandro*). Usually you shout this loudly, but if that might disturb someone, it is better just to exhale strongly without shouting.

---

[133] Tib. hi hing, hu hUM, hUM hri / ཧི་ཧིང་། ཧུ་ཧཱུྃ། ཧཱུྃ་ཧྲི།

Rotating head to the right.

Rotating head to the left.

Nodding backwards and forwards.

47

ii) Life-supporting Wind

Inhale slowly and smoothly through both nostrils.

Focus on the wind entering the central channel through the two side channels.

Then focus on your heart chakra, on the white wish-fulfilling jewel there.

Hold your breath.

When you are ready, re-inhale, then:

Press your left thumb into the base of your left ring finger and close the fingers of your left hand over it to make a *vajra*-fist. Press this fist into your groin, at the top of your left inner thigh. Make a *vajra*-fist with your right hand and 'throw the lasso,' drawing your hand around your head from left to right then throwing your arm out in front of you, opening your fist as you do so.

Repeat this five times.

This is a very strong movement.

Swap sides and repeat.

Then make a *vajra*-fist with both hands, press them into your groin, and rotate your right shoulder back five times. This is also a strong movement. You mainly move your shoulder, but the whole of your upper body moves, too.

Then rotate your left shoulder in the same way.

Repeat this five times.

Exhale slowly and strongly.

The goal is to open the heart chakra and fortify the life-supporting wind.

...g a *vajra*-fist.

thrulkhor. Right side. Do this five times then repeat the whole cycle on the left.

...ing shoulder backwards. Do this five times then repeat the whole cycle on the left.

49

iii) Fire-equalising Wind

Inhale slowly and smoothly through both nostrils.

The wind comes through the side channels into the central channel, and fills all your chakras but you concentrate mainly on the navel chakra, on the three-flamed fire there. It is very hot. Don't be distracted.

Hold your breath.

When you are ready, re-inhale, then:

Place your hands on your hips, thumbs front.

Pull your stomach in and back.

Rotate your stomach towards the right five times, moving your stomach in and out and round at the same time, like giving an inner a massage.

Then rotate towards the left in the same way five times.

Then, sitting straight up, pull your stomach up and in, then down and out, 'rotating' it five times from front to back, up and down.

Exhale slowly and strongly.

This is for the stomach, but it affects all your organs. It is very good for digestion.

ng the stomach towards the right five times.

ing the stomach towards the left five times.

ng the stomach in and up.   Pushing the stomach down and out.

iv) All-pervading Wind

Inhale slowly and smoothly through both nostrils.

The wind comes through the side channels into the central channel and fills your whole body.

Hold your breath.

Visualise a green wind pervading your whole body, like the sun's rays, but focus mainly on your limbs.

Tense your arms and legs, including your buttocks, very, very strongly, and clench your toes strongly, too. Make two *vajra*-fists and place your hands at the top of each thigh, in your groin. Tuck your chin down.

When you are ready, re-inhale, then:

Stretch your left arm straight out, keeping the *vajra*-fist clenched.

Massage down your left arm, on the inside, then up on the outside back to your shoulder. Repeat this five times applying quite strong pressure. When you make the *vajra*-fist, the channels stand out so the massage is more effective. It is similar to when a doctor has to take blood and you need to make a fist to help the veins stand out. This should be a strong fist so that massaging your arms is of great benefit for your circulation. As you do this movement, keep your body tense from shoulder to finger tips, from hip to the tip of your toes.

Swap sides, and repeat another five times.

Then rub both legs strongly with your palms, starting at your thighs and ending at your feet. Repeat this five times.

Then 'shoot an arrow,' towards the left. When you shoot the arrow, lift up your whole upper torso (so that if someone shoots you in the stomach, your lungs and heart would be up out of the way. It's a wide, fluid movement, both arms describing circles). But keep your head looking straight ahead; this exercise is not for your head, it is for your limbs.

Repeat this five times. Then swap sides, and repeat another five times. Exhale slowly and strongly.

...saging the left arm. Do this five times then repeat on the right.

...ssaging the legs. Repeat five times.

...oting an arrow towards the left. Do this five times then repeat on the right.

v) Downward-moving Wind

Inhale slowly and smoothly through both nostrils.

The wind comes through the side channels into the central channel.

Focus on your secret chakra and visualise the blue bellows there. The wind fills up the chakra.

Hold your breath.

When you are ready, re-inhale, then:

Firmly grasp your right knee with both hands and rotate your lower body, from the waist down, strongly to the right, and to the back. Repeat this five times.

Move strongly and, close your lower doors firmly as you rotate to the right, and relax it as you rotate to the left because this exercise works with your lower doors.

Then swap sides, holding your left knee with both hands, and rotating to the left. Repeat this five times.

Then take your left knee with your left hand and your right knee with your right hand, rotate your lower body forwards and to the right five times then backwards and to the left, five times. Close your lower doors for the first half of each rotation and relax it for the second half. Repeat this five times. Keep your chin tucked in slightly.

You are holding your knees mainly for support; you need to move your lower body strongly.

Exhale slowly and strongly.

Thus the practice of the Five Winds is finished.

ng right knee and rotating lower body to the right.
s five times then swap sides and repeat on the left.

ng both knees and rotating lower body to the right.
is five times then repeat towards the left.

7. The Key Point of the Guiding Sounds

བདུན་པ་འདྲེན་པ་སྒྲའི་གནད་ཀྱིས་ཚ་ལམ་སྟོང་བ།

There are three guiding sounds:
i) the long, dignified sound which pleases the *lama*: HEE HEENG.
ii) the sound which makes the *yidam* smile: HU HUNG.
ii) the sound which calls the *khandro*: HUNG HRI.

Whichever one you use, you should shout in such a way that all your inner organs shake, and you should pull your stomach up a little. The sounds should be big, strong and short. But if you are in a public place or if you have many neighbours, it is better just to exhale strongly without shouting, otherwise you might disturb someone.

8. The Key Point of *Tummo* Practice

བརྒྱད་པ་གཏུམ་མོའི་དམིགས་པ་ཏིང་འཛིན་གནད་ཀྱིས་ཚ་སྐྱོན་བསལ་བ།

Visualise a flat triangle of fire, pointing towards your back, inside your central channel at the junction of the three channels.

On top of this flaming triangle, visualise a lotus cushion, a sun cushion, and a moon cushion, each slightly smaller than the one below.

On top of the moon cushion, visualise Degjye Drolma[134], the *tsalung khandro*. The smaller the better – the best is the size of a thin needle. But that is difficult at first.

Generally, she is green, the colour of the wind, but in this case she is red, representing fire. However, if you have a hot disease or it is too hot outside, visualise her as green. If you have a cold disease and if it is cold outside, the *khandro* should be visualised as red.

---

[134] Tib. 'Degs byed sgrol ma / འདེགས་བྱེད་སྒྲོལ་མ།

She is standing in the dancing posture with her right leg raised. She is holding a hooked knife with a *norbu* handle in her right hand, a *kapala*[135] skull cup brimming with *düdtsi*[136] in her left hand. She has a *khatvanga*[137] in the crook of her left arm representing her consort, and a crown ornamented with five skulls on her head. She is wearing bone bracelets and other bone jewellery.

Fire flames behind her. It is extremely hot – if you put an iron ball inside, it will melt immediately – pshhh!

So it is very hot – there is a triangle of fire, and flaming fire behind the *khandro*. Visualise this as clearly as possible, as small as possible.

Inhale slowly and smoothly through both nostrils.

The wind comes through the side channels and enters the central channel at the junction of the three channels, filling the central channel.

Focus on the fire, on the *khandro* with fire behind her. The focus is always here. Then just practise the Lung Practice with Four Aspects, as before.

In this case, re-inhale at least three times.

As the fire burns more strongly, you can visualise the heat rising slowly through your central channel. First it fills the secret chakra, then it comes up and fills the navel chakra, then the heart chakra, then it rises through your throat chakra right up to your crown chakra. If you just focus very strongly on the secret place, on the *khandro* and the fire, then the heat will rise automatically and your whole body will become hot.

If you need protection, focus on the red *khandro*.

When you are ready, exhale strongly, and remain in the Natural State for at least fifteen minutes.

---

[135] Tib. ka pa la / ཀ་པ་ལ།
[136] Tib. bdud rtsi / བདུད་རྩི།
[137] Tib. kha TAM ga / ཁ་ཊཾ་ག།

Red Degjye Drolma.

Green Degjye Drolma.

If your meditation is disturbed by drowsiness, strengthlessness or agitation, then you can visualise a red Tibetan A instead of the *tsalung khandro* on the cushion. In this case, you don't concentrate on fire or heat, you simply focus on the red A. The breathing is the same as for the *tummo* practice above.

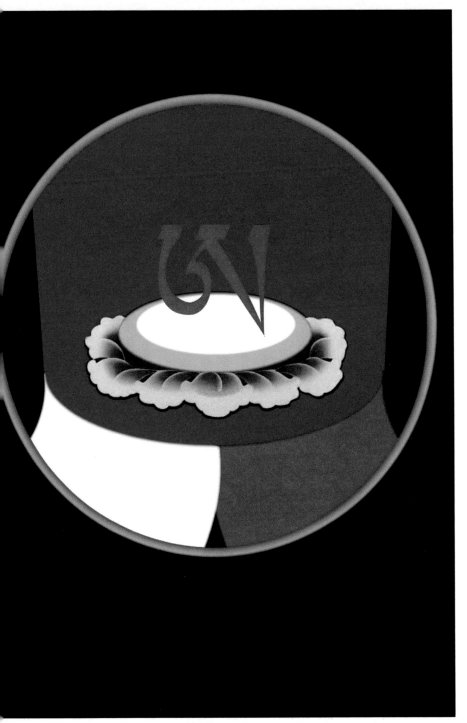

Red Tibetan A.

If your meditation is disturbed by too many discursive thoughts, then visualise a white *thigle* instead of the *tsalung khandro*. In this case, you don't concentrate on fire or heat, you simply focus on the white *thigle*, like a crystal ball. The breathing is the same as for the *tummo* practice above.

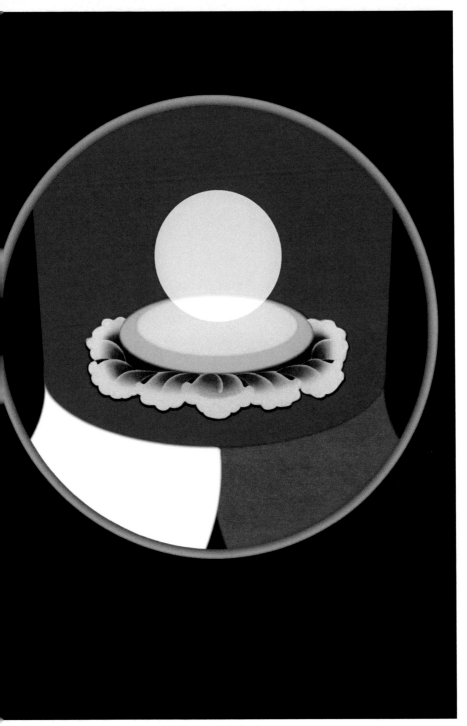

White crystal *thigle*.

If you are in a very cold place, somewhere like the snow mountains of Tibet, and you need to warm up, then just visualise the fire, without the *tsalung khandro*. In this case, your inner fire grows and rises up the central channel a little way, like a fine triangle torma, *ashe*[138]. Focus on that. In this case, the flaming triangle is slimmer and not horizontal but vertical, pointing up the central channel. It is standing on the sun disc with neither lotus cushion nor moon disc.

If your realisation of the Natural State is clear and stable, then focus on the fine pyramid of fire and remain in the Natural State.

---

[138] Or Tib. a shad / ཨ་ཤད། – an upside-down stroke of the Tibetan letter 'a'.

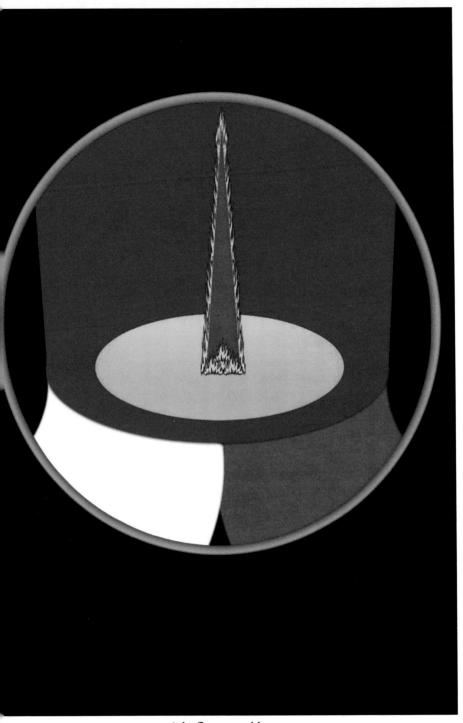

Ashe fire pyramid.

9. The Key Point of the Benefit of Tummo Practice

དགུ་པ་རྩ་རླུང་གཏུམ་མོའི་རྣལ་འབྱོར་ལ་བརྟེན་པའི་ཕན་ཡོན།

If these five winds are in perfect harmony, then you will have a healthy life.

This is written in the Magyu teachings, but also in the *Sorig Bumzhi*[139], *The Four Medical Texts*. These Four Medical Texts explain that all diseases appear from an imbalance of the five winds. Everything depends on wind.

The channels, *tsa*, are also very important. Why? Because the winds move inside them, they come and go through the channels, so if there is something wrong with a channel, if the winds are blocked, then it is very difficult for the wind-energy to circulate through the body. It may be difficult to inhale or exhale, too. So the channels are very important.

As for the *thigles*, in this case *thigle* means the vital essence of the body, so if something is amiss you will have problems.

Through practising *tsalung*, the winds, channels and *thigles* are strengthened and harmonised, so existing health problems subside, and it is difficult for new problems to arise. Your meditation also becomes clearer and stronger.

---

[139] Tib. Gso rig 'bum bzhi / གསོ་རིག་འབུམ་བཞི།

Concluding Remarks

I do a cycle of these nine key points every day. If you practise each of the Practices of the Five Winds once, do the *tummo* breathing at least three times. If you practise each *tsalung thrulkhor* more than once – if you are in retreat, for instance – then you should do the *tummo* practice more than three times.

Sometimes you can simply relax your mind and do the Practice of the Five Winds, the five *tsalung thrulkhor*, without any visualisation. This is also very beneficial, especially if you are dull, or lazy. Then you can do this practice as a physical exercise, one movement after the other in quick succession, without any visualisation and without the guiding sounds.

If your meditation is dull and you have a few minutes spare, you can do this practice and it will make you very alert.

It is best to take this practice slowly and gently at first. If you are not familiar with breath retention, you can train gradually, without doing the *thrulkhor* exercises but just focussing on the visualisation and increasing the length of time you can hold your breath. You can increase your capacity little by little, a few seconds at a time. Don't force or strain yourself.

Similarly, if some of the movements in the *thrulkhor* exercises feel strange or uncomfortable – for instance, if you feel dizzy while rotating your head – you can sit in a relaxed way and gently practise the movement without holding your breath to familiarise yourself with it. When you feel more comfortable with the movement, you can combine it with visualisation and breath retention.